INVASION OF THE SHAPESHIFTER

ACT ONE
SCENE ONE

NARRATOR: Maurice Toombs and Jack Morpeth are in the hallway of Jack's old house.

Fade in FX of howling gale and wind lashing against window.

MAURICE: *(determined)* I must see what is going on in your cellar, Jack. You owe me one look, you promised.

JACK: *(frightened)* Not tonight, Maurice, not tonight.

MAURICE: I must look. I want to find out what is happening down there. Somebody has to do something.

JACK: *(becoming very agitated)* The night is wild, things aren't right.

FX: *A howl of wind and the cellar door crashes open.*

MAURICE: Something is going to happen tonight. I have to find out!

JACK: No, no, don't be a fool! You have a wife and two little ones. What'll they do without you? It's too dangerous, Maurice.

MAURICE: *(impatient)* Out of my way, Jack Morpeth, you're a coward and you know you are.

JACK:	*(desperate)* No, don't go down there.
MAURICE:	Out of my way!
FX:	*Sound of struggle at the top of the stairs. Footsteps as Maurice descends the stairs.*
JACK:	*(timidly following Maurice)* Take care, my friend.
FX:	*A clap of thunder.*
MAURICE:	Power cut!
JACK:	No - it's the evil in the cellar. Keep away from the chest, Maurice. Keep away.
FX:	*Creak as lid is lifted.*
MAURICE:	I have found something. It's just as we thought. Aaagh!
FX:	*Silence, followed by a crash of thunder.*
JACK:	Maurice, I cannot see you. Maurice? Maurice, you fool.

SCENE TWO

Fade in pop music from a radio.

NARRATOR:	Ten years have passed. Almer and Rowena, thirteen-year-old twins, are sitting in Almer's bedroom. They can hear their mother singing, downstairs.
FX:	*Mum singing along with pop tune.*

4

ROWENA:	Mum's happy. She's got an excuse to celebrate, it's her birthday.
ALMER:	She'll want us out of the way, so she can throw one of her wild parties.
ROWENA:	She keeps telling us she changed when Dad disappeared, but that's ten years ago. I can't even remember what Dad looks like, can you, Almer?
ALMER:	Dad? No, we were too young when he did a runner. I sometimes think he's in Florida, sitting on some sunny beach. What do you think?
ROWENA:	I used to dream that he was in terrible difficulty and he was calling for help. I thought he was far away and he wanted to get back to us, but he was trapped.
ALMER:	He's in Florida! It's we who are trapped, in this rotten old town. And Mum; she's changed so much. She used to be such a good mum. Life seemed so secure. Now she only wants parties. She mostly ignores us. It's as if Dad left and evil entered this town!
FX:	*A loud knock on the front door*
MUM:	*(Off)* Almer, Rowena, Grandad Jack's arrived. He wants you two to play chess with him tonight.
ROWENA:	*(to Almer)* Grandad Jack?
ALMER:	Told you, she wants us out of the way. Race you downstairs!

FX:	*Sound of falling and laughter.*
JACK:	*(He is not the man he was. His hair is grey and his breath is wheezy)* I've come to take you two away from this sinful place ... for a quiet evening of chess and draughts.
MUM:	Go on then you two, out of the house. My guests will be here soon.
NARRATOR:	The twins walk towards Jack's house. The old man cannot keep up with them.
FX:	*Footsteps crunching on gravel.*
ROWENA:	Why is Jack so good to Mum? It's almost as if he owes her a great debt. He isn't our real grandad, he's no relation. What hold has Mum got over him? What is the mystery?
ALMER:	I don't know, but I think it has something to do with his house. How would you describe Jack's house?

ROWENA: *(without hesitation)* Foreboding.

ALMER: That is the very word, foreboding.

ROWENA: I hate Jack's house and garden, they are so creepy. Do you think the house is haunted?

ALMER: Oooh! *(making a ghostly noise)*

ROWENA: Ahhh, what was that? Oh Almer, don't do that!

ALMER: I remember once, when Jack was drunk, he said a strange thing. We'd been playing chess. He suddenly leaned across the board, scattering chess pieces everywhere, and said -

ROWENA: *(interrupting)* What did he say, Almer?

ALMER:	He told me I had to be brave if I wanted good to win through. He called me Maurice, Dad's name. He said 'You have to be brave, Maurice, otherwise you will never contain what is in that old cellar.'
ROWENA:	Did he? That's creepy!
ALMER:	He frightened me. I haven't told you until now because …
ROWENA:	*(prompting her brother)* Because?
ALMER:	I want to see what's in old Morpeth's cellar. The cellar is the clue to Dad's disappearance, I am sure of that!
ROWENA:	The old man was probably rambling.
ALMER:	*(determined)* I need to find out!
ROWENA:	*(She looks behind her. She sees that Jack is catching them up.)* Shhh!
JACK:	Here we are, Toombs twins. My house, my castle, my fortress. You are welcome! Follow me!
NARRATOR:	The twins enter Jack's house. He takes them into his dark, damp kitchen and they sit around a wooden table. Jack is drinking whisky, he and Almer are playing chess.
FX:	*Loud ticking of clock.*
JACK:	*(sounding increasingly tired and befuddled)* You wouldn't like a drop of whisky yourself, boy?
ALMER:	No way.

ROWENA:	*(excited)* Almer, you have one of Grandad Jack's knights and one of his bishops. You must win!
JACK:	*(yawning)* And I only have two of his pawns. Your brother is beating me, Rowena.
FX:	*A sudden crash of thunder.*
ROWENA:	Funny, the weather forecast is good. Is there always a storm over this house?
	(Jack Morpeth grunts)
ALMER:	Check!
FX	*Clink of bottle and pouring sound.*
JACK:	*(depressed)* You're allowing me to drink myself to defeat, boy!
ALMER:	I'm not interested in winning a game of chess. I'm interested in the -
ROWENA:	Shhhh ...
JACK:	Now ... I'll move my king out of check. I'll ...
FX:	*Snoring noises.*
ROWENA:	He's asleep at last. Well done, Almer.
FX:	*Another crash of thunder. The cellar door bangs open.*
ALMER:	Quick Rowena, down the steps.
FX:	*A howl of wind and a wailing sound.*

	The bulb has gone. We'll have to walk down the cellar steps in almost total darkness!
ROWENA:	What a disgusting smell down here. It's like mouldy cheese and rotting peat all rolled into one.
ALMER:	It's only the damp. My trainers are soaked. The floor is flooded. Perhaps old Jack was talking about a burst pipe when he said our Dad couldn't contain what had been released in the cellar! A burst pipe? Water? *(disappointed)*Is that the mystery of the cellar?
ROWENA:	No, look - at the far end!
ALMER:	*(alarmed)* What, Rowena?
ROWENA:	Can't you see it? A shadowy grey figure.
ALMER:	The shape, it's beckoning me towards the chest.
ROWENA:	Now it's gone.
FX:	*The heavy tread of an old man.*
JACK:	Don't make the same mistake as Maurice. Don't let more evil out!
ALMER/ ROWENA:	*(shocked)* Grandad Jack!
JACK:	Upstairs, to your bedrooms. At once!

SCENE THREE

FX: *Fade in school sounds, voices and books being dropped.*

NARRATOR: The twins are in school. Their form teacher, who also teaches them geography, is in a foul mood.

ROWENA: *(whispering to Almer)* I just can't stop thinking about last night. Can you ever forget Grandad Jack sitting, guarding the door to his cellar like a dragon guards its hoard of gold?

ALMER: And when he dropped us off at school this morning, he told us we could never stay with him again, ever! That was too harsh.

ROWENA: He has something big to hide. We must discover the cellar's secret, whatever the -

MR LUSHINGTON: Quiet, Rowena Toombs. *(He looks coldly at Almer.)* It's you again, Almer Toombs. I bet you were making your sister talk.

ALMER: No, sir.

MR LUSHINGTON: Don't no sir me, Toombs. If you're so clever, name an Australian state.

NARRATOR: Almer names all the Australian states, and annoys Mr Lushington, who does not like his pupils to be as clever as he thinks he is.

SCOTT: Toombs thinks he's so clever.

MR LUSHINGTON:	Yes Scott, when I was at school, I knew how to deal with Almer's sort. I used to beat them up.
FX:	*The bell sounds.*
MR LUSHINGTON:	Alright you lot, out of my classroom.
FX:	*Noise of chairs scraping, students leaving classroom.*
ROWENA:	*(to Almer)* Have you heard the joke about the teacher who went to weight watchers? He wanted to lose a stone of ugly fat.
ALMER:	No.
ROWENA:	He lost the fat, but he's still ugly.
ALMER:	*(laughing)* That sounds like Lushington.
SCOTT:	Clever Almer Toombs. Too clever Almer Toombs.
FX:	*Thump of Almer being hit in the midriff.*
MR LUSHINGTON:	Get your carcass off the floor, Toombs, you make the place look untidy.
ROWENA:	*(helping Almer to his feet)* They're still bullying you. When will it ever stop?
ALMER:	What can I do against a giant like Scott Gully?
ROWENA:	There are hundreds of stories about brave heroes who killed horrible giants.

ALMER: I don't think the school would thank me for bringing a sling into the playground. And if I did, I'd probably find the wrong stone and it wouldn't work.

ROWENA: Who'd believe one of the bullies was a teacher? I saw Lushington wink at Scott Gully. This town's evil. What was it Jack said? He said ... he said ...

ALMER: 'Don't let any more of the evil out.'

ROWENA: We have to get back into his cellar. We must think of a plan.

SCENE FOUR

NARRATOR: The twins are back home from school. They have not seen their mum since the party.

ROWENA: The house looks like it's been trashed. Oh I hate the smell of stale cigarettes and beer.

ALMER: Let's have some fresh air.

FX: *Window is opened.*

MUM: *(spoken in a monotone)* Hello you two. Make yourselves some tea, will you? I don't feel like anything just yet.

ALMER: *(sarcastically)* A good party was it?

MUM: *(ignoring Almer)* There is a nice piece of ham in the fridge. Now, I really must go and lie down. I've a splitting headache.

14

FX:	*Mum walks slowly upstairs*
ROWENA:	Let's look on the bright side, we get to make our own tea.
ALMER:	*(sighing)* I just wish Dad was here.
ROWENA:	*(recognising that Almer is fed up)* What's green and can jump a mile a minute?
ALMER:	*(shrugs his shoulders)* Am I supposed to guess?
ROWENA:	A grasshopper with hiccups!
ALMER:	*(sarcastic)* Ha, ha. *(he thinks)* Get the torch, Rowena.
ROWENA:	Why?
ALMER:	Let's skip tea. We'll grab some crisps and cake, then take a look at Morpeth's cellar. I have a plan.
NARRATOR:	The twins walk up the lane to Jack Morpeth's house.
FX:	*Owl hoots. Footsteps.*
ROWENA:	Everything is so creepy here. The trees in the garden are like tall soldiers guarding Jack's secret. *(gasps)* Did one of the trees move, Almer?
ALMER:	It's certainly spooky.
NARRATOR:	They creep up to the front gate.
ROWENA:	Something evil is inside this house, I'm sure of it.

15

ALMER:	*(tense)* Remember the plan. As long as we stick to the plan.
ROWENA:	I know what to do. I won't let you down.
NARRATOR:	Rowena picks up some stones, and throws them at a window.
FX:	*Stones hitting glass.*
NARRATOR:	Almer runs towards the house and hides behind a tree, near the door.
FX:	*A heavy door opens.*
NARRATOR:	Jack staggers out of the doorway. He can hardly keep upright and he is clutching a whisky bottle.
JACK:	*(shouting into the darkness)* Go away, go away pests.
ROWENA:	*(to herself)* I hope the plan works. *(to old Jack, in a voice not her own)* Mr Morpeth, I have something to show you, out here.
FX:	*Sound of an old man walking along a gravel path.*
JACK:	Who are you? What do you want?
NARRATOR:	While Jack is away from the door, Almer runs into the house.
ALMER:	*(to himself)* She's leading him away from the house. Good girl, Rowena. Let's hope you can double-back without Old Jack recognising you. Now for the cellar door – and what lies below!

16

NARRATOR: Ah, the poor innocent children, if only they knew what they were doing!

SCENE FIVE

NARRATOR: Rowena finds Almer waiting for her in Jack's kitchen.

ROWENA: *(out of breath)* Old Jack is still looking for naughty boys who throw stones. He's wandered out into the lane. Shall we go down?

FX: *Cellar door creaking open.*

ALMER: Did I really see anything in the cellar? Was that figure above the old wooden chest a trick of the light, or my imagination? I'm scared, but we have to find out.

ROWENA: Take a deep breath!

ALMER: We could be done for trespassing if Old Jack finds us here.

ROWENA: *(bravely)* Let's get going!

ALMER: Careful. Don't slip in the dark. Where's my torch?

(Silence)

FX: *Jack's heavy tired steps are clearly heard along the pathway outside.*

ALMER: Wow! It's so wet down here. My trainers feel like soggy rice puddings already.

ROWENA: Mine, too. I feel like a demented duck!

ALMER:	*(fingers to lips)* Shhh. Be serious for once. There – over by the far corner – above the chest.
ROWENA:	Is it a shadow, an outline? I'm not sure.
ALMER:	*(relieved)* Just a trick of the light.
NARRATOR:	*(afraid)* Is there something above the chest? Something hovering? A genie guarding its master's gold – or a genie with a lamp?
ALMER:	*(He takes a deep breath and splashes his way to the chest.)* Here goes!
NARRATOR:	Almer reaches the chest. His fingers clutch the lid. All he has to do is pull the lid back. He glances behind him. At the top of the stairs stands old Jack Morpeth. He is still clutching his bottle of spirits. Jack is shaking his head in disbelief.
JACK:	*(to Almer)* No, No, No! Do not let the evil out too soon. The time is not right. Your dad would not have wanted this. Isn't there enough evil in our town already? You know how the boys behave. Touch the chest at your peril.
NARRATOR:	The misty shadow above the chest is growing and becoming real. It's grey and wispy. It looks like a shadow that's wandered the spirit world for centuries.
ROWENA:	*(to Almer)* I'm scared.
FX:	*Almer opens the heavy chest lid. There is deep laughter from inside.*

ROWENA:	*(screams)* Almer … Look at what you have released … it's monstrous.
FX:	*More deep laughter.*
ROWENA:	Oh what a hideous-looking beast. Covered in scales …
ALMER:	With blood-red eyes …
ROWENA:	Evil in its face …
ALMER:	And smelling of decay … like a grave …
NARRATOR:	The creature gradually changes shape. The Shapeshifter laughs, a high-pitched human laugh.
JACK:	Another Shapeshifter!
NARRATOR:	The creature is now a tall slim man, in his early forties. He is dressed in a smart blue suit. He is smiling. His smell is still grave-like. He bows to the children, deliberately mocking them. He splashes through the water, heading for the stairs.
JACK:	*(from the top of the stairs)* Almer, what have you done?
FX:	*Noise as the man-creature pushes past Jack and is gone into the night.*
JACK:	What have you unleashed into this world? Where has he gone? *(to the twins)* Stay – *(his hands shake)* I will tell you the full story! This town changed when Maurice, your father, opened the chest and released some evil - a very small shapeshifter, that we later caught

and confined. That meant we contained the evil. The chest, given to me by my grandfather, has a link with an evil world. Your father was sucked into the chest and is trapped in that world! You have released a large shapeshifter that will cause a great deal of trouble to this town.

FX: *Sinister sounds – such as threatening music, ghostly noises or owl hoots and screeches.*

SCENE SIX

NARRATOR: The twins are in the school grounds, taking a short-cut home across the playing fields. They are both feeling very frightened. They meet their English teacher, Miss Eagleton.

MISS EAGLETON: Shouldn't you two be at home? Time is moving on.

ALMER & ROWENA: Yes, Miss.

MISS EAGLETON: Well, you can cut through the playing fields for once.

ALMER: Why are the school lights on, this time of night, Miss?

MISS EAGLETON: *(sadly)* We've had rather a tragedy. We've had to convene an emergency session of the school governors. Our poor headmaster, Mr Ellis, has suffered a heart attack.

ROWENA: Oh no. Poor man.

MISS EAGLETON: Luckily, the Education Authority have provided us with a relief teacher – a man called Mr Knight.

(Miss Eagleton watches the twins walk across the playground. She shouts after them)

Take care!

ROWENA: Yesterday, if Jack had told us Dad was trapped in some other planet, I would not have believed him. But that was yesterday!

ALMER: Tonight is another world and it's as if we've travelled years in one hour.

(They arrive home and ring the bell. Mum opens the door.)

FX: *Sound of bell and door opening.*

MUM: *(in good spirits)* Welcome home, you two. We have a lodger, Mr Knight. He's your relief headmaster.

NARRATOR: The twins look past Mum and see the Shapeshifter who emerged from the chest in the cellar.

FX: *Scream from the twins.*

SCENE EIGHT

NARRATOR: The twins are in the local park. It is near midnight. Rowena is sitting on a swing and Almer is standing beside her.

ALMER: I have to make Knight go back to his evil world. *(pause)* I must be the stupidest boy in the universe. If only I'd listened to old Jack Morpeth.

ROWENA: There isn't a single reason why Knight should even dream of going back inside that chest in Jack's cellar. Why should he? He's spent ages trying to break into our world. He's not likely to suddenly think 'Right, I've made a mistake, I'll slip back to the cellar and snuggle down in the chest and wait for a few hundred years to pass.'

ALMER: Not likely!

ROWENA: I hate to admit this... but we need adult help.

ALMER: Who can help us?

ROWENA: I don't know. *(suddenly frightened)* Mum's alone... with the Shapeshifter ... We have to get back.

ALMER: And do what?

ROWENA: *(panicky)* I don't know what we can do, but we can't leave her alone.

ALMER: I think I have a plan, but I need your help. This is what we'll do: you pretend you are ill and skip school. While our new headmaster is in school, you sneak into his room at home and see if you can find anything. A good plan, eh?

ROWENA: Dangerous, but worth a try! Now let's get back home, Almer.

(Later)

MUM: *(dishevelled)* What time do you call this? Upstairs, you two. Now! *(moves away)*

KNIGHT: *(to Almer)* First, I need your help. You'll come to no harm if you're on my side.

(Knight smiles at Almer.)

ALMER: But....

KNIGHT: You have helped the cause already. You shall be rewarded when we take over.

NARRATOR: Knight begins to change into the monster he really is. With a concentrated effort, the monster becomes Knight again.

ALMER: But....

KNIGHT: You shall be rewarded once the victory is ours.

ALMER: Rewarded? Victory ours?

KNIGHT: *(smiling)* Don't worry about anything. See you in the morning!

FX: *Knight walks upstairs. Mum comes into the room.*

MUM: I like our lodger. He's a real dish. And think of the money! You're so lucky having such a handsome young headmaster!

ACT TWO SCENE ONE

NARRATOR: The next day. Almer is in school. Mr Lushington is behind his desk, grinning.

MR LUSHINGTON: Directions from our glorious new headmaster. You lot have to line up outside my room until I call you. Got it? *(all the class nod)* You walk in, single file, and stand behind your desks. No talking - or I'll send you to Mr Knight. Got it? Understand? *(the class nod)* It's called positive discipline. You do anything wrong, you get punished. And I approve!

NARRATOR: Outside the classroom windows, Jack Morpeth is lurching along the path.

FX: *Boys sniggering.*

MR LUSHINGTON: Ignore what is happening outside!

FX: *Morpeth bangs on the classroom window with his fist.*

JACK: *(Through the open window)* Children, your new headmaster is a monster – created from the chaos of the Universe.

FX: *Laughter.*

He may look human but he's a … a… Shapeshifter!

BERNIE: *(laughing)* Yeah, and I'm from Mars!

JACK:	*(very loud)* Your great and glorious headmaster is a …
FX:	*Footsteps as Lushington strides across the classroom and closes the window.*
MR LUSHINGTON:	Scott Gully – find Mr Brick, the caretaker. Tell him to remove the drunk from these premises.
SCOTT:	Yes, Sir.

(There is chaos in the classroom. Bernie Forman is sprawled across the floor, laughing. The new headmaster, Mr Knight, strides in, furious)

MR KNIGHT:	What is going on here? *(to Bernie Forman)* You – outside my study at once! What's the meaning of this din, Mr Lushington?
MR LUSHINGTON:	An old drunk was causing a disturbance – the fellow that lives in the gloomy house near the woods. What's his name … Morpeth.
MR KNIGHT:	*(agitated)* I see. *(to the class)* Settle down. I want you silent.
	(Silence as Mr Knight leaves the room)
SCOTT	*(to Almer)* Heh, you. Where's Rowena?
ALMER:	*(remembering the lie)* She's not very well – a migraine.
NARRATOR:	Later, Bernie returns to the class. He has altered. His hair seems to have turned white. His eyes are dulled.
SCOTT	Bernie looks as if he's lost his life-force. What has Mr Knight done to him?
NARRATOR:	Later, at break. Bernie's friends notice how he has altered.
SCOTT:	What did old Knight do to you, mate?
GARY:	Yeah, tell us!
BERNIE:	*(in a flat, staccato voice)* He turned into a monster. His eyes were as red as blood. His claws touched me. I remember nothing else.

FX	*Laughter.*
SCOTT:	Yeah, yeah. You're having us on!
GARY:	*(imitating Jack Morpeth)* Children, your headmaster is a monster – created from the chaos of the Universe.
FX:	*Laughter, and whimpering from Bernie.*
SCOTT:	Bernie, what's he done to your hair, mate? Your hair's as white as snow.
GARY:	Come on Bernie, you're acting like a zombie. Let's have a kick around, show us your footie skills. *(Bernie slumps forward)* Bernie, Bernie?

SCENE TWO

NARRATOR:	It is breakfast time, the following day, at the Toomb's household.
ALMER:	Bernie ended up in the medical room.
ROWENA:	Heh! What gets bigger the more you take away?
ALMER:	This is not the time for joking …
ROWENA:	A hole! We're in one and it's getting bigger by the hour.
ALMER:	We'll have to visit Morpeth again.
ROWENA:	*(shudders)* No. I'm not going near his house. Not today!

ALMER:	Why not? *(thinks)* Yesterday, did you sneak into Knight's room – as we planned? Did you find anything?
ROWENA:	*(in a trance)* Nothing. I found nothing. Had a migraine.
ALMER:	*(shocked)* No you didn't have a migraine. That was part of the plan, to keep you away from school so you could snoop around Knight's bedroom.
ROWENA:	My head hurt all day. I was ill, in bed.
ALMER:	No!
ROWENA:	*(appears to come out of her trance)* Come on, Almer. We'll be late for school.
NARRATOR:	At school the twins are talking together. Mr Lushington spots them.
MR LUSHINGTON:	The terrible twins talking again!
SCOTT:	Send the Toombs twins to our headmaster, Sir.
GARY:	Yeah!
NARRATOR:	Mr Lushington wants, above all else, to be popular and to stay in with the cool gang.
MR LUSHINGTON:	Out, you two, out of my room.
ROWENA:	*(tearful)* You're not fair, sir. You always pick on Almer, just because he's clever.

MR LUSHINGTON: *(roars)* Rebellion! Out, both of you! To the headmaster's study!

NARRATOR: As Almer leaves the classroom, he turns and sees Bernie staring at him with vacant eyes, tears streaming down his face.

SCENE THREE

Outside the headmaster's study.

ROWENA: Bernie? He's usually insensitive to anything.

ALMER: *(pointedly)* But he's been inside Knight's study.

ROWENA: Knight! He came home yesterday at lunch-time.

ALMER: And?

ROWENA: *(shakes her head)* I don't know! I can't remember. I was in his room, I'd picked the lock. Just as we had planned. Then -

ALMER: Yes?

ROWENA: *(worried)* That part of yesterday is just a blank. Then I was in bed, with a sickening headache.

ALMER: Knight can't have done you too much harm. You haven't ended up like Bernie.

Miss Eagleton appears

MISS EAGLETON:	You two waiting for Mr Knight?
ALMER:	Yes, Miss.
MISS EAGLETON:	Mr Lushington sent you here? *(the twins nod)* I thought so. Come with me to my classroom.
	(The twins follow Miss Eagleton into her classroom)
	I want you to talk to a very important school governor. Come on!
FX:	*Opening of classroom door.*
MISS EAGLETON:	Let me introduce you both to Mr Noble. He is our new school governor. Mr Noble, meet Almer and Rowena Toombs.
MR NOBLE:	Splendid. I hear you are a clever fellow, Almer Toombs.
MISS EAGLETON:	*(quickly)* As is Rowena. She has a great imagination.
Mr NOBLE:	Good, good. We have a competition for gifted children. Bright Challenge! Now, who's your form teacher?
ALMER:	Mr Lushington, sir.
MR NOBLE:	Yes, yes. *(pause)* I will withdraw you from Mr Lushington's lessons.
FX:	*The bell goes.*
MR NOBLE:	Ah – time flies. I shall see you two again.

(The twins walk out of Miss Eagleton's room. Mr Lushington stumbles towards them. He is holding a mug of strong and steaming tea.)

MR LUSHINGTON: *(sarcastic)* Going somewhere boy?

ALMER: No sir!

MR LUSHINGTON: Don't worry, Toombs. I'll get even, and I don't care how!

SCENE FOUR

NARRATOR: The twins are standing outside Jack Morpeth's house. It appears even more gloomy than usual.

ALMER: I want our Dad back and I know Jack is hiding something from us. But I released the Shapeshifter. He'll go mad with us!

ROWENA: You made me bunk off school to sort this out. We're here to see Morpeth, let's get on with it!

FX: *Door knocker. Door creaking open.*

JACK: Ah! Maurice Toombs's children. Come on in, come in!

(He bows)

ROWENA: *(to Almer)* Yuck, the smell.

ALMER: *(to Rowena)* He hasn't washed for days.

JACK: Sorry children – I haven't shaved. Quite a grey stubble, eh? *(He rubs his chin)* End of the line for humanity, eh?

ALMER: What...?

JACK: *(cutting Almer off)* Mankind thought himself so proud, so clever, but we're losers. We haven't been around as long as the dumb dinosaurs were. *(laughs deeply)* Nothing can be done. Fact is, your dad tried to stop 'em. But once one is out, they'll find a way to invade.

33

ROWENA:	What? Who?
JACK:	Clever man, your dad. Too clever! Worked for an intelligence agency. Bet you didn't even know! Sheila - your Mum - she never knew.
ALMER:	Dad – but…
JACK:	*(interrupting)* Nothing's as it seems. These Shapeshifters inhabited a dying planet. They travelled without shape or form. They travelled through time and space, searching for a home. My grandad, a clever man, trapped them and confined them to that chest in my cellar. He kept a close eye on the evil beings while he lived. And then the burden fell on me. Me? Mine was the burden of the Universe!
ROWENA:	Then what happened? Something did happen, didn't it, Grandad Jack?
JACK:	The Shapeshifters created a worm-hole in space, from their planet to ours. They learned, over time, how to leak out of the chest. They learned how to take human shape. It was only a matter of time before… before they escaped, but to be substantial, the chest lid had to be opened by somebody who was from our world. Your father was given the task to sort out the problem.
ALMER:	And?
JACK:	He failed. He released a Shapeshifter and he was captured. I didn't help him. My cowardice haunts me to this day.
ROWENA:	*(kindly)* Don't blame yourself, Grandad.

| JACK: | Grandad? I am not worthy of the name. *(to Almer)* You released one Shapeshifter, the others will follow. *(suddenly angry)* Now go. Our days are numbered. I want to be alone, left in peace. Go! |

SCENE FIVE

Almer and Rowena sneak back to school. It is lunch-time.

MISS EAGLETON:	*(out of breath)* Almer, Rowena. I've been looking for you everywhere. I am so sorry!
ALMER:	Sorry?
MISS EAGLETON:	*(close to tears)* Mr Knight assembled all the school governors this morning. He has dismissed Mr Noble. He told the governors Mr Noble will be replaced by one of his friends.
ROWENA:	*(to Almer)* Another Shapeshifter!
MISS EAGLETON:	Mr Noble has driven away in his car – and gone with him is the 'Bright Challenge'. I'm handing in my immediate resignation.
ROWENA:	Please, Miss Eagleton, don't go. You can't!
MISS EAGLETON:	*(tearful)* I'm sorry!
NARRATOR:	The twins walk slowly away. As they do so, they feel a tap on their shoulder.

MR KNIGHT:	*(smiling)* Haven't I done well? But I need your help. Only human beings can lift the chest lid to release my friends… my kind.
ALMER:	*(quickly)* I will never help you again.
MR KNIGHT:	Tut, tut. We shall see. Lost your memory for a time, Rowena? Oh, and your favourite teacher, Mr Lushington *(there is menace in Knight's voice)* is my new deputy headteacher. Mr Collis fell downstairs this morning. He's had a nasty little accident. *(in a high-pitched voice)* And, after you've helped me, I'll give you a little present … your father released, unharmed. If not – your mother will end up like Bernie.
	(Mr Knight walks away)
ROWENA:	*(relieved)* He's still alive!
ALMER:	*(staggering, almost in a faint)* Help me!
ROWENA:	I'll take you to Jack's house, it isn't too far.
FX:	*walking on gravel path*
ALMER:	We've got to get to Jack's cellar. I'm going in, after Dad.
ROWENA:	You can't!
ALMER:	I must…I have to, it's the only way.
NARRATOR:	The twins arrive outside Jack Morpeth's house.
FX:	*The sound of an ambulance siren.*

36

POLICEMAN: Move away, children. No onlookers.

ALMER: *(quickly)* He's our Grandad.

ROWENA: Well practically … I mean … almost.

POLICEMAN: He's not a pretty sight. Move off!

ALMER: What's happened to Mr Morpeth? Please tell us.

POLICEMAN: *(Relenting)* The old man's dead. Torn apart by a large, vicious animal … least, that's what it looks like to me. Not a lot left of the old fellow. Mutilated, he is!

(The shocked twins move away)

SCENE 6

NARRATOR: Later, snow is falling fast, blanking off the town from the outside world. The twins are still in the lane, near Jack's house. A policeman is guarding the front door.

ROWENA: *(shivering)* We can't stay here all night. We'll die of exposure.

ALMER: If we go home, we'll end up zombies – like Bernie Forman.

ROWENA: Being a zombie will do fine!

ALMER: *(trying to keep Rowena's spirits up)* Heard the one about the crocodile?

ROWENA: No.

ALMER: I'll tell you the answer… but I'll make it snappy.

FX:	*Attempted laugher from Rowena.*
NARRATOR:	Could there be help at last? Trudging through the thickening snow is the tall, thin figure of Mr Noble.
MR NOBLE:	Ah, the twins. We need to get into that cellar.
ALMER:	But there's a policeman standing outside old Jack's house…and Jack is dead.
MR NOBLE:	Yes, yes. I guessed as much. The policeman should present no problem.
NARRATOR:	Mr Noble marches up to the policeman and talks to him. The policeman stands aside. Mr Noble beckons the twins forward.
MR NOBLE:	Come on, no time to lose.
ALMER:	*(catching up)* Who are you?
MR NOBLE:	All will be revealed, later. Down to the cellar, quickly!
FX:	*Sounds of Mr Noble and Almer walking down the steps and wading through the water.*
ALMER:	Where's Rowena?
MR NOBLE:	Quick, no time to lose. Almer, I was your father's boss.
NARRATOR:	Just at that moment Mr Knight, Mr Lushington, Scott and Gary arrive. They are at the top of the stairs. Rowena hangs limply on Mr Knight's arm.
MR KNIGHT:	Ah yes, Almer Toombs, please do open the chest.

(Mr Noble and Almer spin round)

ALMER: What have you done to Rowena?

MR LUSHINGTON: I told you I'd get even, Toombs.

MR KNIGHT: Open the chest, or these bullies will hurt your sister.

SCOTT: I've waited a long time for this, Toombs. And now the grown-ups will let me do what I want.

GARY: He can do what he wants, Toombs.

FX: *Scott and Gary laugh.*

MR KNIGHT: *(soothing)* You do want to get Daddy, don't you?

MR LUSHINGTON: Open the chest boy, now!

SCOTT: *(bangs his fist with his open palm)* Or else.

FX: *Scuffling, as Scott pushes Rowena, and she slips down some steps.*

ALMER: *(tearful)* No! You're not to hurt my Rowena. You've changed her. What have you done to her?

MR NOBLE: *(In a booming, powerful voice)* I know who you are, Norman Knight. You are here to invade. Go back to your place in the Universe.

39

FX:	*Sinister snarling from Mr Knight.*
NARRATOR:	Mr Knight shapeshifts into a monster. Mr Lushington gasps and falls down the steps. The two boy bullies are terrified.
SCOTT:	*(whispers to Gary)* Come on, let's get out of here.
GARY:	Yeah.
FX:	*Footsteps as the boys rush back up the stairs.*
MR LUSHINGTON:	*(to Mr Noble)* Forgive me, please forgive me. I didn't know what I was doing. I've been a fool.
MR NOBLE:	*(with command and authority)* Be gone, and don't come back to this town ever again.
MR LUSHINGTON:	*(stuttering nervously)* No, no. Never. I swear it.
MR NOBLE:	Yes, yes. Now go! *(He shines his torch on Knight the Shapeshifter – who looks sick.)* What's the matter, monster? Can't you shapeshift? Used up all your strength frightening the policeman away and hurting that poor girl? *(He walks over to Rowena and helps her to her feet.)* Return to your corner of the Universe Shapeshifter! *(Mr Knight nods meekly.)* Almer, open the chest.
NARRATOR:	Knight the Shapeshifter struggles to turn into the monster he really is.

FX:	*Roaring and bellowing.*
MR NOBLE:	Oh, is that all you can do? *(to Almer)* You see, this creature does not truly exist in our world, if we don't want it to – he can't harm me, because I'm not afraid.
ALMER:	*(gaining some of Mr Noble's courage)* Go, Monster!
MR NOBLE:	Shrink into that chest!
NARRATOR:	The monster does as Mr Noble commands.
	(to Almer) You will find Mr Ellis returning as your headmaster, soon. Miss Eagleton will be here in a moment, to look after Rowena. *(He takes a mobile phone from his pocket.)* And we need to follow Knight into his world. Tonight, you and I travel to a strange place – to find your father.

SCENE SEVEN

NARRATOR:	Mr Noble and Almer are whirling through a dark void. They are floating past stars, galaxies and supernovas – or so it appears to Almer. They slow down and land on what appears to be a floating cloud.
FX:	*Music to suggest travel through time and space.*
MR NOBLE:	Welcome to the furthest corner of the Universe!

Suddenly the Shapeshifter is before them.

FX:	*A snarling sound.*
MR KNIGHT:	I was not really in your world. Now you are weak in mine. I will give you Maurice Toombs, but I want his daughter, Rowena. Fair exchange? One for one!
ALMER:	My father or my sister?
MR KNIGHT:	Exactly!
ALMER:	Dad or Rowena.
MR KNIGHT:	The choice is yours.
MR NOBLE:	Don't you realise you have lost?
MR KNIGHT:	Lost? Why don't you creep back to your world and await my return? I and my kind will conquer, one day.
MR NOBLE:	Be reasonable, Shapeshifter. One for one, you have just told us. Give this boy his dad and take a greater prize…Me!
MR KNIGHT:	That does appeal. Oh, the torture you'll enjoy here.
Mr NOBLE:	Yes, yes. I understand. Just get on with it, take me – release Toombs.
ALMER:	No, no. That's not fair.
NARRATOR:	Almer is taken up in a gust of wind and is spinning in a void.
ALMER:	Keep away from me, Knight.
ROWENA:	It's alright, Almer. You're back with us.

ALMER:	Mr Noble? What have they done to you? Your face is quite different. And the red marks around your wrists. You are limping.
MAURICE:	Mr Noble? No, I'm Maurice. And you are…Almer? My son?
ALMER:	Dad! Oh Dad, what have they done to you? You look so…
MAURICE:	I am alive, Almer…alive! That's the most important thing. And I have work to do. I must destroy the worm-hole through space that these creatures have created.
MISS EAGLETON:	All the evil will then go – this town will become what I believe it once was!
NARRATOR:	A shadowy form emerges from the chest and becomes Mr Noble.
ALL:	Mr Noble!
MR NOBLE:	Those puny Shapeshifters could not hold me for long. Come Maurice, there is work to be done.
MAURICE:	Yes, boss.
MR NOBLE:	But first, you must be reinstated with your family.
ALMER:	What will Mum say?
MAURICE:	We must always be vigilant. These creatures must never return.
FX:	*Fade in music to suggest all is well, fade out music.*

NOTES ON PRODUCTION

This play could be used for classroom reading, or as a radio play, recorded on to tape, with appropriate sound effects (FX).

INVASION OF THE SHAPESHIFTER

ACTIVITIES
ACT ONE: SCENE ONE

Freeze-framing
In small groups, freeze-frame the moment when Jack is trying to keep Maurice away from the chest in the cellar. What will their expressions be? Will Jack be afraid or angry? Will Maurice appear cautious, determined or thoughtful? You decide!

Improvisation
Maurice has disappeared. In small groups improvise a scene in which Jack has to tell Maurice's wife and friends that something has happened to him. What will Jack say to convince people that Maurice has simply run away? How will everyone react?

Recording
How can you tell that this play is written as a radio script? In groups of three or four, record the first two scenes. Use sound effects and changes of voice for dramatic effect. Play the tape back and decide how you can improve the recording. What worked well and what might need changing? When you are happy with the result, play the recording to the rest of the class. Discuss each group's recordings

Writing
In pairs, take turns to imagine you are a policeman investigating the sudden disappearance of Maurice Toombs. Note down all the evidence you have gained so far and report back to your superior officer. Finally, write up your notes as a police report.

Discussion and writing

In small groups, imagine you are senior members of staff at the school. You have evidence that there are a number of incidents of bullying at your school. You have heard about Almer's plight. Discuss ways of stopping the bullying through teacher attitudes and form an anti-bullying policy. Decide what goes into the policy and how it would work. One of you might need to keep notes.

Improvisation

You are the school governors interviewing Mr Knight for the position of headmaster. He needs to convince you that he would make a good relief headmaster. He will need to lie and bluff his way through this interview. Nobody must discover he is a shapeshifter. Take it in turns to be Knight.

Writing

Almer and Rowena are writing a joint diary about all that has happened to them so far. They will want to include all the important events they have been involved in, which might include:
The game of chess and Almer's attempt to reach the chest.
School, with Mr Lushington and the bullies.
Almer and Rowena's return to Jack's house.
The Shapeshifter.
Mr Knight as a lodger.
The plan

Miss Eagleton has been asked to write a confidential report on Mr Lushington. Write a report stating why you think Mr Lushington would not make a good teacher.
Invent your own shapeshifter and write a description.

Scriptwriting

The play is meant for radio. Script a scene or two that you particularly like for television or theatre. Remember that in radio, the audience cannot see the action, but in theatre or on the television, they can.

Will you still need a narrator? If not, what directions would you need to write so that the actors know what you want them to do? Would you need visual directions?

ACT TWO: SCENES ONE TO FOUR

Improvisation
In pairs, pretend you are Bernie and Mr Knight. What does the shapeshifter do to Bernie that turns him into a zombie? Act out this scene.

In pairs, you are Mr Knight and Rowena. How does Mr Knight stop the plan and discover all the information he needs to know? How does he make Rowena ill? Rowena remembers nothing, how does Knight destroy her memory about the above events?

Mime
You are the shapeshifters and you are creating a wormhole in space. Mime the aliens doing this and mime them creeping into the chest. Finally, mime their release as Maurice Toombs opens up the chest.

Writing
Mr Lushington has to write a report to Mr Knight about the appearance of the drunken Jack Morpeth. He also indicates in the report the reasons why his class are so badly behaved.

ACT TWO: SCENES FIVE TO SEVEN

Discussion
In small groups, decide how you think Jack was killed and how the police discovered his death. You will need to be inventive, but there are some clues within the play.

Mime

Mime Mr Noble and Almer whirling through a darkening void. Try and use mood music and sound effects to create atmosphere.

Improvisation

Develop and act out scene seven, as Almer meets his long-lost father.

Writing

Prepare a local radio or tv news report on the death of Jack Morpeth. Interview Mr Knight, Mr Noble and Almer and Rowena. Find out their different views on the death of Jack.

Maurice Toombs has to write a report for Mr Noble about his time with the shapeshifters. He also needs to write about his rescue. Use your imaginations - Maurice was living on an alien planet for over a decade!

Reflecting on the play

Think and talk about what makes this play a science-fiction drama. Do you enjoy science fiction? Say why or why not. What other examples of science fiction do you know of? Think about books, radio, television and films.

Think about the surnames in the play. Can you guess why Maurice was called Toombs or the Shapeshifter was named Knight? Are any other names in the play significant?